Tangled Tongue Twister Fun

a GAME of LAUGHS for ALL AGES!

J. W. Meyer
Adriana L. Meyer

Copyright © 2021
Tangled Tongue Twister Fun
A Game of Laughs for All Ages

Original text and original artwork Copyright © Justin W. Meyer and Adriana L. Meyer

IMMUTABLE PUBLISHING

All rights reserved. No part of this publication may be reproduced, stored in a retrieval system, or transmitted in any form or by any means, electronical, mechanical, photocopying, recording, or otherwise, without the prior permission of the copywrite owner and the above publisher of this book.

Any similarity of the images in this book, to the appearances of real animals, munchkins and goblins, is purely coincidental.

ISBN: 978-1-7329415-2-6 (paperback), 978-1-7329415-3-3 (epub)

Publishing and Design Services: MartinPublishingServices.com
Graphic Art: Aiva Šmugā

Dedicated to the

Wonderful Mother Lover Hugger

Rules of the Game

1. Smiles, laughs and fun are required.

2. Sit together with family and friends.

3. Count the number of people. Triple that number and **add 1**. This is how many tongue twisters you will use for the game.

4. For ultimate enjoyment, keep the game moving at a **fast** pace.

5. The youngest person reads the first tongue twister and **quickly** memorizes it. About 8-12 seconds.

6. Close the book.

7. **By memory**, recite the tongue twister as fast as you can five times in a row.

8. The other players will judge for acceptable speed and accuracy. Be fair.

9. If a mistake is made, quickly pass the book to the next person and **keep the game moving**.

10. The next person gets a chance to memorize and recite the original tongue twister.

11. You get a point when the tongue twister is correctly repeated five times. Now, pass the book and move on to the next tongue twister.

12. The person with the most points at the end is the winner!

13. For maximum satisfaction, start another game!

14. As you improve, adjust time expectations for memorization and reciting.

Super Chicken
Bean Machine

Never **Rather**
Clever Blather

Nibble Drabble
Dribble **Babble**

Some See She Saw

Slick Slide Slip Splat

Sassy Uncle Monkey Scandal

Yammer Blabber
Gutter Clubber

**Snap Clap
Drip Flap**

Jibber Jelly Butter Belly

Dash Bash Crash Smash

Fuzzy Rubber Bunny Biscuits

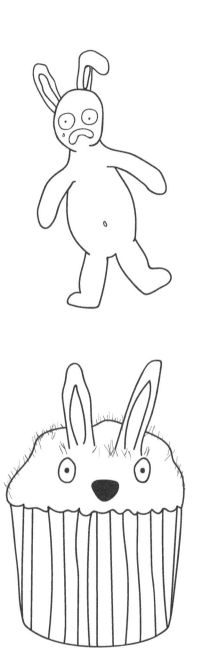

Bitter Bubble

Water **Boil**

Splatter **Place**

Paint Brace

Cut Some
Fresh Shoots

Chunky Lumpy
Chubby Bumpy

Speckle

Splatter

Gecko

Smatter

Grab Stack Wrap Wrack

Art Champ Doodle Stamp

Sleepy Green Thumping Queen

Ponder **Plunder** Under **Thunder**

Defiant
Violent
Wiggling
Duck

Cello Pick-Up
Fickle Stick-Up

Stop Abrupt
Become Irrupt

Perfectly **Plump** Pasta Platter

Giggle Tickle **Bagel** Belly

Mustache
Munchkin
**Backslash
Pumpkin**

Jelly Buddy Funny Fellow

Wonderful Huggable Loveable Nudge

Bindle ━━━━━━━━━━
━━━━ Beaker ━━━━━
━━━━━━ Bundle ━━━
━━━━━━━━━ Bushel

Flower Flap
Tiger Slap

Sticky Panda Candy Wrapper

Book **Baby**
Glue **Master**

Camper Picture
Handle **Stamper**

Better Butter Bread **Biter**

Boring **Snoring Motor** Pony

Bump Set Spike Teddy

Yummy Licking Bacon Fingers

Squawker Talker Stumpy Walker

Bell Backpack
Door Lamp

Pretty Blue Bubble Globes

Laughing
Wacky
Witch
Donkey

Greenish Pinkish Maybe Brown

Sneaky Social Media Marketing

Roof Top Soup Shop

Spindle Widget
Kindle Fidget

Cactus Berry Feather Fairies

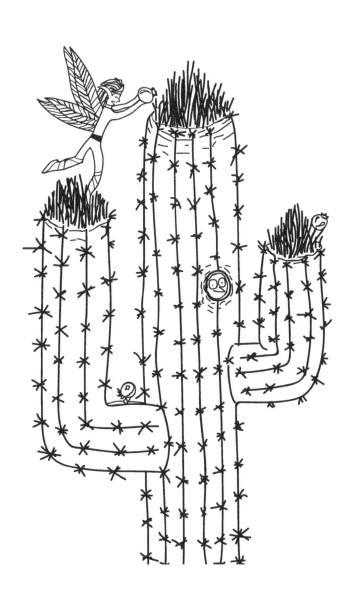

Grubby
Knuckle Cowboy
Buckle

Shoulder
Leather Blender
Welder

Giggle
Laugh
Tickle
Wiggle

Huge
Flying
Carpet
Starship

Mini Sitting Baby Kitty

Dusty **Musky**
Winter Husky

Hungry Rumble
Tummy Grumble

Silver Sable
Jumper Cable

Salty

Sugar

Coco

Burger

Big Black **Bulging** Blowfish

Oat Bran Muncher Muffin

Scuttle Under Bungle Blunder

Crystal Thistle
Pistol Missile

Humble ugly
Rugby Tumble

Stinky Yellow

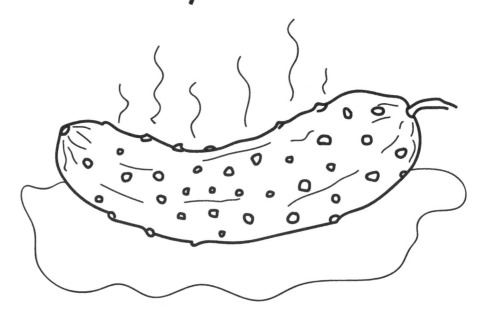

Sticky Pickle

Random Dripping Candle Shambles

Steamy Wonky Scamper Banter

Powdered Chowder Power Hour

Armless Caramel Camel Farmer

Weird Honking Dog Barking

Plumpy Plunger
Toilet Puppy

Lucky **Sour**

Berry **Boy**

Splish Splash Puddle Slash

Edible Uncurling Fiddlehead Ferns

Squishy Little Drippy Shrimp

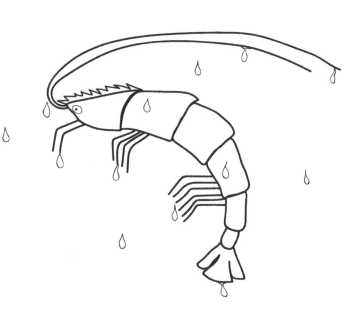

Dribble Batter
Bumper **Crop**

― Cookie ―
― **Crumble** ―
― **Tummy** ―
― Grumble ―

Beefy Bulging Blubber Bucket

Flinging Bubbly Booger Chunk

Pitter Patter Spider Splatter

Stinky Duty
Booty Butt

Funky **Salty**
Sloth Sausage

Frail Tail
Dragon Trail

**Better Button
Zipper Sweater**

Fluffy Fuffy Fuzzy Bat

Dizzy Bitty Bitter Beads

Fresh Smoked String Cheese

Wonderous Whimsical Flipping Giant

Mainly Many Misty **Money**

SPRING FED TROUT STREAM

53

Free Blurry Curry Fritters

Holy Bounding Rolling Boulders

Cheap Creaky Squeaky Sneakers

She Says She'll Share

Dumpster Robbing Garbage Goblin

Shake Your Socks Off

Crunchy Granite Rubble Puncher

Gargle
Bargain
Jargon
Margin

Wiggle
Mingle
Hamster
Jingle

Yucca Mucky Ducky Pool

Several Helpless Selfish Shellfish

Summer
Gale
Flapping
Sail

Billowing
Puffy
Pillow
City

Bulky Barfing Bog Monster

Scary Very
Frightening
Lightning

Thin Riddle
Schnibble Nibble

Muddy Buddy Dirty Boys

Crispy Crusty Celery Puffs

SILLY LITTLE SHEEP STUFFY

Icky Funky **Grundy** Cluster

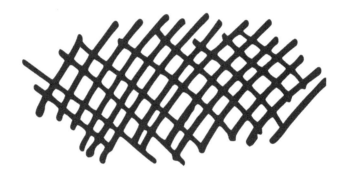

Salvaged **Useless** Lumber **Chunks**

Trite **Minded**
Sparkle Sprite

Golden Moldy
Porridge **Storage**

BUSY BUZZY BEE BUDDY

Candy Coated Chocolate **Crunchies**

Perfectly Magical **Moss Clusters**

Road

Cone

Skin

Tone

Chicken

Egg

Inspection

Center

Big
Round
Clown
Frown

Mushy
Frozen
Toaster
Nuggets

yellow
Belly
Lilly
Liver

> Jump Hop
> Skip Bump

Five-ish
Six-ish

ACKNOWLEDGEMENTS

Thank you to everyone who shares in the effort to spread fun and enjoyment with this book. This means you!

We also want to express special appreciation to those who made it possible to turn our words and drawings into a complete book.

Publishing and Design Services: MelindaMartin.me

Graphic Art: Aiva Šmugā, aiva.smuga@gmail.com

I would also like to recognize my daughter, Adriana, for all the courage and hard work that she invested into this project.

ABOUT THE AUTHORS

J. W. Meyer lives in Europe where he divides his time between family, writing and traveling. He always enjoys goofing around and having fun with people at gatherings. It is one of his firm beliefs, that life should be filled with plenty of laughs, and overflowing happiness!

Adriana is 11 years old and lives in Europe with her family. She loves animals, nature and having fun outdoors. Adriana is a budding fantasy reader who is easily drawn into an exciting story. This is her first book.